SWING
Playalong *for* Tenor Saxophone

WISE PUBLICATIONS
London/New York/Paris/Sydney/Copenhagen/Madrid

Exclusive Distributors:
Music Sales Limited
14-15 Berners Street, London W1T 3LJ, England.
Music Sales Pty Limited
Units 3-4, 17 Willfox St, Condell Park, NSW, 2200, Australia.

Order No. AM959618
ISBN 0-7119-7485-3
This book © Copyright 1999 by Wise Publications.

Book design by Michael Bell Design.
Music arranged by Paul Honey.
Music processed by Enigma Music Production Services.
Cover photography by George Taylor.
Printed in the EU.

CD produced by Paul Honey.
Instrumental solos by John Whelan.
Engineered by Kester Sims.

Your Guarantee of Quality:
As publishers, we strive to produce every book to
the highest commercial standards.
The music has been freshly engraved and the book has been
carefully designed to minimise awkward page turns and
to make playing from it a real pleasure.
Particular care has been given to specifying acid-free, neutral-sized
paper made from pulps which have not been elemental chlorine bleached.
This pulp is from farmed sustainable forests and was
produced with special regard for the environment.
Throughout, the printing and binding have been planned to
ensure a sturdy, attractive publication which should give years of enjoyment.
If your copy fails to meet our high standards,
please inform us and we will gladly replace it.

Saxophone Fingering Chart

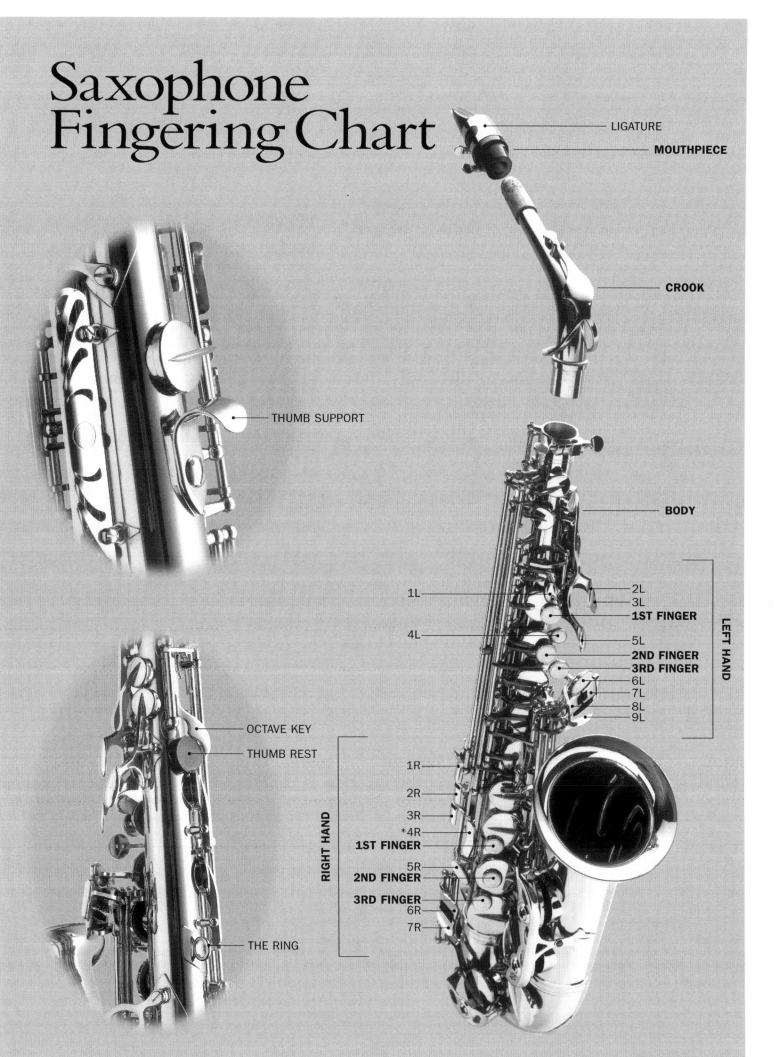

LIGATURE

MOUTHPIECE

CROOK

THUMB SUPPORT

BODY

1L
4L

2L
3L
1ST FINGER
5L
2ND FINGER
3RD FINGER
6L
7L
8L
9L

LEFT HAND

OCTAVE KEY

THUMB REST

1R
2R
3R
*4R
1ST FINGER
5R
2ND FINGER
3RD FINGER
6R
7R

RIGHT HAND

THE RING

* Not fitted on some saxophones

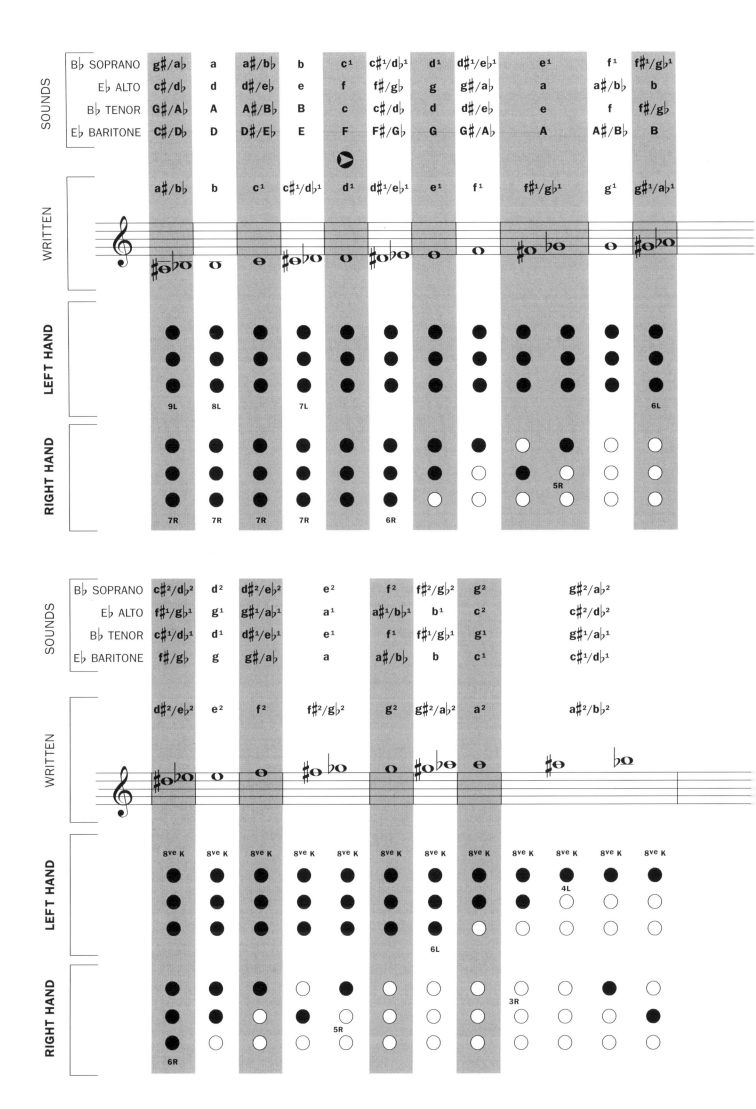

Indicates the lower limit of the best playing range

g¹   g#¹/ab¹   a¹   a#¹/bb¹   b¹   c²

c¹   c#¹/db¹   d¹   d#¹/eb¹   e¹   f¹

g   g#/ab   a   a#/bb   b   c¹

c   c#/db   d   d#/eb   e   f

a¹   a#¹/bb¹   b¹   c²   c#²/db²   d²

4L · 3R · 2R · 8ve K · 8ve K · 7L · 7R

a²   a#²/bb²   b²   c³   c#³/db³   d³   d#³/eb³

d²   d#²/eb²   e²   f²   f#²/gb²   g²   g#²/ab²

a¹   a#¹/bb¹   b¹   c²   c#²/db²   d²   d#²/eb²

d¹   d#¹/eb¹   e¹   f¹   f#¹/gb¹   g¹   g#¹/ab¹

b²   c³   c#³/db³   d³   d#³/eb³   e³   f³

8ve K · 8ve K · 8ve K · 8ve K · 8ve K · 8ve K · 8ve K · 8ve K · 8ve K · 8ve K

3L · 2L 3L · 2L 3L · 1L · 1L

2R · 1R · 1R

Indicates the upper limit of the best playing range

Ain't Nobody Here But Us Chickens

Words & Music by Joan Whitney & Alex Kramer

Bright swing

I'm Getting Sentimental Over You

Words by Ned Washington
Music by George Bassman

Moderate swing

rall.

Flying Home

By Benny Goodman & Lionel Hampton

Medium swing

Jump, Jive An' Wail

Words & Music by Louis Prima

Bright swing

(straight quavers)

Hit That Jive Jack

Words & Music by John Alston & Campbell "Skeets" Tolbert

19

Swing That Music

Words & Music by Louis Armstrong & Horace Gerlach

Is You Is Or Is You Ain't My Baby?

Words & Music by Billy Austin & Louis Jordan

Moderate swing

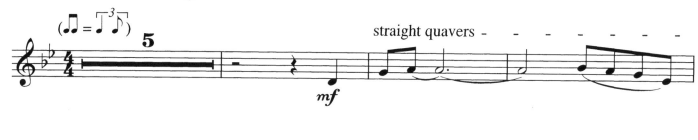

poco rall.

Perdido

Music by Juan Tizol
Words by Harry Lenk and Ervin Drake

Easy swing

Tuxedo Junction

Words & Music by Buddy Feyne, Erskine Hawkins, William Johnson & Julian Dash

Moderate swing

Zoot Suit Riot

Words & Music by Steve Perry

02/14 (189749)